The FOOLISH MAN SYNDROME

THE DIFFERENCE BETTWEEN SUCCESS AND FAILURE

Copyright © 2018. All Rights Reserved.

No part of this publication may be reproduced, distributed, or transmitted in any form or by any means, including photocopying, recording, or other electronic or mechanical methods, or by any information storage and retrieval system without the prior written permission of the publisher, except in the case of very brief quotations embodied in critical reviews and certain other noncommercial uses permitted by copyright law.

Why You Should Read This Book

success in life depends on how we think, either you think big and succeed or you think small and vice-versa

This book will show you how your thinking influence your life and why you need to think big, not small.

Table of Contents

Why You Should Read This Book

Table of Contents

Chapter 1. Introduction

Chapter 2. The act of thinking small VS The act of thinking small

Chapter 3. How thinking big can influence your road to success

Chapter 4. How to Develop the Habit of Thinking Big

Chapter 5. The Barriers to Thinking Big

Chapter 6. How thinking small influence your success

Chapter 7. how thinking small compared you to the likes of grasshoppers,sloths etc

Chapter 8. How thinking big compared you to the likes of lion, wolf, eagles,tigers etc

Chapter 9. How the way you think (either big or small) determine how your life turns out

Chapter 10. How to change the way you think

chapter 11.

chapter 12.

chapter 13. conclusion

introduction to thinking

Thinking occurs as automatically as blood circulation in the human body and perhaps during both the wakeful hours and while we sleep too, and hence the difficulty in defining it. Perhaps we should define the kinds of thoughts or thinking we are concerned with in this post.

The brain weighs about 3 pounds & has three parts - the cerebrum (which is of primary interest here),.the cerebellum, and the medulla oblongata (the brain stem). It bears repetition that the oxygen is very high consumption of energy compared to any other organ. Not surprisingly, it occupies most of the skull. The link at the top of this paragraph, though the context is different, does provide useful information on the brain.

The cerebrum is the part that is responsible for thinking, feeling, remembering, and problem solving and hence is the primary organ that is considered in this post on thinking.

From Wikipedia, thought is described as - Thought can refer to the ideas or arrangements of ideas that result from thinking, the act of producing thoughts, or the process of producing thoughts. Although thought is a fundamental human activity familiar to everyone, there is no generally accepted agreement as to what thought is or how it is created. Thoughts are the result or product of spontaneous acts of thinking.

This definitions gives clues as to what is a better way to think

Thought (also called thinking) – the mental process in which beings form psychological associations and models of the world. Thinking is manipulating information, as when we form concepts, engage in problem solving, reason and make decisions. Thought, the act of thinking, produces thoughts. A thought may be an idea, an image, a sound or even an emotional feeling that arises from the brain.

Thinking allows humans to make sense of, interpret, represent or model the world they experience, and to make predictions about that world. It is therefore helpful to an organism with needs, objectives, and desires as it makes plans or otherwise attempts to accomplish. Perhaps this is how sciences came to exist and could be conveyed to future generations

Thinking is the cognitive activities you use to process information, solve problems, make decisions, and create new ideas. You use your thinking skills when you try to make sense of experiences, organize information, make connections, ask questions, make plans, or decide what to do.

There are several different types of thinking or ways to think.

Creative thinking – refers to the ability to conceive new and innovative ideas by breaking from established thoughts, theories, rules, and procedures. It involves putting things together in new and imaginative ways. Creative thinking is often referred to as "thinking outside the box."

Analytical thinking – refers to the ability to separate a whole into its basic parts in order to examine the parts and their relationships. It involves thinking in a logical, step-by-step manner to break down a larger system of information into its parts.

Critical thinking – refers to the ability to exercise careful evaluation or judgment in order to determine the authenticity, accuracy, worth, validity, or value of something. In addition to precise, objective analysis, critical thinking involves synthesis, evaluation, reflection, and reconstruction. And rather than strictly breaking down the information, critical thinking explores other elements that could have an influence on conclusions.

Concrete thinking – refers to the ability to comprehend and apply factual knowledge. It is about thinking of objects or ideas as specific items, rather than as a theoretical representation of a more general concept. It involves thinking only on the surface, always literal, and to-the-point.

Abstract thinking – refers to the ability to use concepts to make and understand generalizations then relating or connecting them to others items, events, or experiences. It involves paying attention to the hidden meanings thus allowing you to observe and understand theories and possibilities.

Divergent Thinking – refers to the ability to generate creative ideas by exploring many possible solutions in an effort to find one that works. It involves bringing facts and data together from various sources and then applying logic and knowledge to solve problems or make decisions. It starts from a common point and moves outward in diverging directions to involve a variety of aspects or perspectives.

Convergent thinking – refers to the ability to put a number of different pieces or perspectives of a topic together in some organized, logical manner to find a single answer. It involves focusing on a finite number of solutions rather than proposing multiple solutions.

Sequential (linear) thinking – refers to the ability to process information in orderly prescribed manner. It involves a step-by-step progression where a response to a step must be obtained before another step is taken.

Holistic (nonlinear) thinking – refers to the ability to see the big picture and recognize the interconnectedness of various components that form the larger system. It involves expanding your thought process in multiple directions, rather than in just one direction, and understanding a system by sensing its patterns.

Types of thinking can be divided into several opposing categories;

Small Thinking vs. Big Thinking

The act of thinking small The act of thinking small

The act of thinking small	The act of thinking big
Concrete Thinking	Abstract Thinking
Convergent thinking	Divergent thinking
Analytical Thinking	Creative Thinking
Sequential Thinking	Holistic Thinking

Concrete Thinking vs. Abstract Thinking

Concrete thinking refers to the thinking on the surface whereas abstract thinking requires much more analysis and goes deeper. Concrete thinking will only consider the literal meaning while abstract thinking goes deeper than the facts to consider multiple or hidden meanings.

Concrete thinking refers to the process of comprehending and applying factual knowledge. It involves only those things which are visible and obvious allowing any individual to observe and understand. Abstract thinking goes beyond all the visible and present things to find hidden meanings and underlying purpose.

Example:

A concrete thinker will look at the flag and only sees specific colors, marking, or symbols that appear on the cloth. An abstract thinker would see the flag as a symbol of a country or organization. They may also see it as a symbol of liberty and freedom.

Convergent thinking vs. Divergent thinking

Convergent thinking involves bringing facts and data together from various sources and then applying logic and knowledge to solve problems or to make informed decisions. Convergent thinking involves putting a number of different pieces or perspectives of a topic back together in some organized, logical manner to find a single answer.

The deductive reasoning that the Sherlock Holmes used in solving mysteries is a good example of convergent thinking. By gathering various bits of information, he was able to put the pieces of a puzzle together and come up with a logical answer to the question of "Who done it?"

Divergent thinking, on the other hand, involves breaking a topic apart to explore its various component parts and then generating new ideas and solutions. Divergent thinking is thinking outwards instead of inward. It is a creative process of developing original and unique ideas and then coming up with a new idea or a solution to a problem

Analytical Thinking vs. Creative Thinking

Analytical thinking is about breaking information down into its parts and examining those parts and their relationship. It involves thinking in a logical, step-by-step manner in order to analyze data, solve problems, make decisions, and/or use information. Creative thinking, on the other hand, refers to conceiving new and innovative ideas by breaking from established thoughts, theories, rules, and procedures. It is not about breaking things down or taking them apart, but rather putting things together in new and imaginative ways.

Example:

An analytical thinker may look at a bicycle to determine how it works or what is wrong with it. A creative thinker may look at the same bicycle and think of a new way to make it faster or a new way to use it.

Sequential Thinking vs. Holistic Thinking

Sequential thinking is processing information in orderly prescribed manner. It involves a step-by-step progression where the first step needs to be completed before then second step occurs.

If a = b, and b = c, then a = c

Holistic thinking, on the other hand, is about seeing the big picture and recognize the interconnectedness of various components that form larger systems. It involves expanding your thought process in multiple directions, rather than in one direction, in order to understand how everything connects. Holistic thinkers want to understand the patterns and how thing connect to each other.

Holistic Thinking

Example:

When assembling a table, a sequential thinker would follow the step-by-step directions. A holistic thinker would want to see or mentally visualize how the table would look when it is completed.

How thinking big can influence your road to success

It All Begins with a Single Thought...

The one major factor that separates the most successful people from the rest begins with a single thought. This single thought — if cultivated — grows over time into the empowering habit of thinking big that eventually takes over this person's psychology, and propels them towards the achievement of their goals and objectives.

We must however keep in mind that over years this single thought is analyzed, criticized and condemned by others. People believe that this thought is impossible, improbably and undeniably unimaginable. They say that the thought is unorthodox and bordering on crazy. And so this single thought must overcome great obstacles, setbacks, problems and difficulties before it can realize its full potential. After all, this single thought understands that in order to grow BIG and expand, that it must accept the harsh realities of life and respond by growing long and strong roots that will support its tremendous weight as it stretches towards the sky. Yes, this single thought knows very well indeed that to think big, is to do big.

How to Develop the Habit of Thinking Big

Just imagine a single snowflake falling from the night sky. By itself it has no hope of changing the world. However, this single snowflake has BIG ambitions and BIGGER ideas. It realizes that it needs to gather together other snowflakes in order to grow BIGGER and STRONGER. And so it decides to fall on top of the highest mountain peak where it interlocks with other like-minded snowflakes. There it waits and waits for the wind to blow and the ground to shake, eventually transforming this single snowflake into one of the most powerful and ferocious forces on earth: A Rampaging Avalanche! And to think that all this started with a single snowflake who dared to think BIG.

Think BIG About...

The first step towards becoming a big thinker involves incorporating the habit of thinking big into every aspect of your life. You must therefore begin to think big about:

• Daily tasks, projects and objectives.

• Your contributions to the world and others.

• Your capacity to think creatively and outside the box.

• Your capacity to think problematically, think critically and flexibly.

• Your capacity to provide value to others.

• Your capacity to overcome any obstacle and challenge that is thrown your way.

- Your capacity to stretch your imagination and the possibilities of your current circumstances.

- Your life's purpose and goals.

Thinking big requires that you think globally about the problems that are confronting your reality. Thinking big requires that you see these things from a wider and far reaching perspective by asking yourself:

- How could this potential solution change the world?

- How could this idea revolutionize my industry?

- How could the answer to this problem solve a global issue?

You must think big without any reservations and without any hesitation in order to contribute more, learn more, become more and stretch yourself and your own abilities beyond their current psychological limitations.

Think Like a Child

At times thinking big isn't easy to do from our limited perspective. We are who we are, and thinking big just might not be a part of our nature. It's something that's difficult to imagine, let alone do. However, there is a way around this that naturally shifts our perspective and makes things a little more fun.

The key to shifting your perspective and developing the habit of thinking big involves stepping outside of yourself and into another persona — essentially becoming someone you are not, yet someone who will help you see things a little BIGGER, better and far more creatively. You could therefore begin thinking big like a:

• Child who has a curious nature and only sees possibilities in amidst turmoil.

• World renowned musician or artist who has an uncanny ability of creating something out of nothing.

• Professional athlete who has the will to persist and overcome any obstacle standing in their way.

• Noble prize winning scientist who meticulously works through BIG problems in small ways.

• Billionaire entrepreneur who knows no limitations in thought or action.

Step into any of these people's shoes, and you will immediately gain a different perspective about your life and the circumstances that are confronting your reality. You will immediately begin to think more clearly, creatively and problematically, which will help you break down the walls that are preventing you from thinking bigger than you have ever thought before.

In order to think big you must think from the perspective of having no limitations and no fears. It's as though life is conspiring in your favor, breaking down all walls and obstacles that are standing in your way, thus releasing your unlimited potential to develop the habit of thinking big, acting big, and doing bigger things than you ever thought were possible.

Developing the habit of thinking big on a daily basis requires a little work and effort. It's not something that will happen overnight, but it is something that will happen over-time as you apply the following big thinking strategies consistently and meticulously.

Cultivation is the Key

Thinking big consistently and effortlessly will come over time. Like any habit, it requires us to develop a plethora of supporting habits that will help us to think big far more effectively.

Empowering Language

The language you use on a daily basis is simply a reflection of your thoughts. If your words are riddled with complaining, worrying and criticizing your life circumstances, then you can expect that your life will undoubtedly be a direct reflection of these words. If on the other hand you begin using empowering words and phrases that are focused on solutions, ideas and on expanding possibilities, then your life will also be a reflection of this type of language.

Big Ideas, Plans and Goals

When setting goals and lay down plans of action don't settle for safety. Think instead of goals that will help expand your comfort zone, push your limits and stretch your imagination — freeing your mind to think big. Life is after all too short for anything else.

Forward Thinking

Thinking big requires forward thinking. Big thinkers think several steps ahead, several moves in advance and several years into the future. They understand that life is simply like a game of chess.

If you do not have the ability to think several moves ahead, then you haven't as yet successfully cultivated the habit of thinking big.

Solution Oriented Thinking

Thinking big is about finding solutions, answers and ideas that will break down the problematic walls that are standing in your way.

Solution oriented thinking involves asking effective questions that will expand possibilities and open ourselves to alternative perspectives that we never considered before.

Indispensable Qualities

Thinking big requires us to cultivate several key qualities and traits that will enable us to think bigger and better than ever before about our life and circumstances. These qualities include passion, courage, optimism, persistence, discipline and enthusiasm.

Unshakable Belief

Thinking big requires a set of unshakable beliefs that magically convince you that whatever you can conceptualize in your mind, you can realize in the physical world. Hence you must believe that...

- When I envision it, I believe it...

- When I believe it, I do it...

- When I do it, everything becomes possible...

Relish Time for Thinking

In order to think big you must first find the time to think proactively about your circumstances. Most people unfortunately don't have this privilege. They simply don't have the time and tend to constantly react to the events and circumstances in their lives. They never actually take the time to STOP and think proactively about solutions and ideas that could make their life easier and solve the problems confronting their reality.

Those who cultivate the\ habit of thinking big understand that the more often they piece these puzzles together the more proficient they will become at solving future unexpected problems that may rudely show up at the worst possible time.

Challenge Weaknesses

Weaknesses are simply things that we have failed to address and consistently focus on over a lifetime. In other words, they are things that we have neglected — and what you don't use, you will lose. Therefore weaknesses should not be seen as limitations, but rather as opportunities for change.

Those who cultivate the habit of thinking big understand that by challenging their weaknesses they naturally strengthen their ability to deal with the unexpected events and circumstances that life throws their way. Likewise they understand that challenging weaknesses adds to their arsenal of skills and resources that they have on hand to help them attain their BIG goals and objectives.

Strengthen Willpower and Resilience

BIG goals and objectives are only achieved by those with the willpower and resilience to keep on moving forward when everyone else has stopped dead in their tracks. Those who think big clearly understand this, and they therefore strengthen their willpower and resilience on a daily basis even when performing the smallest of tasks.

Ask BIG Questions like a Child

Those who think big ask BIG Questions consistently and persistently until the right answer comes to mind. They ask:

- How can I do this better than anyone else?

- How can I think more creatively about this?

- How can I take this to another level?

- How can I think even bigger?

Gather Required Resources

Those who think big realize that thinking big is only the first step that leads to BIG change. They know that to conceptualize a BIG idea is one thing, but to actually bring this idea into reality is completely another ballgame. They therefore strategically gather all the necessary resources, tools, knowledge and support — in advance — that they need to bring their BIG ideas into the physical world.

Build Systems and Processes

Thinking big isn't easy, and that is why it's important to streamline the process as much as possible by building effective systems that will enable you to build your ideas, accelerate decision making and support your creativity.

Constantly Make Bold BIG Decisions

Big thinkers take BIG risks and make bold and BIG decisions on a daily basis that others may not openly support. However, big thinkers understand that their ability to think big allows them to see things from a far wider perspective that others cannot. And for that reason they are also independent thinkers who don't base their decisions on people who only think in small and minuscule ways.

Take Calculated Risks

Those who think big are not unrealistic thinkers who take crazy risks. Big thinkers are smart thinkers who make sure to weigh up the consequences of their decisions thoroughly before taking action.

Take Proactive Action

Those who cultivate the habit of thinking big but do not act are only dreamers. To think big you must act big and move towards your goals and objectives in a thought-provoking meticulous way each and every single day with consistency.

Set Goals Beyond Your Comfort Zone

Thinking big and setting goals that are beyond your comfort zone goes hand-in-hand. In fact, the size and the degree of difficulty of obtaining your goal will provide you with a good indication of how BIG you are thinking at any particular moment. However, we must of course keep in mind that setting goals that are too far beyond our reach is actually counterproductive. If these goals are not attained, then it could lead to stress, worry, fear, procrastination and a plethora of other limiting emotions and behaviors.

Your goals must be believable, achievable and must effectively follow the SMART FOR ME goal setting method.

Set Challenging Time-frames for Objectives

Some goals might seem easy to achieve on the surface. However, if you fiddle around with the time-frame a little bit, you will find that even the easiest of goals can become somewhat challenging.

Those who think big clearly understand that in order to keep themselves on target, motivated and moving quickly, that they must continuously test themselves and their ideas. And this involves setting challenging time-frames that test their limits and stretch their comfort zones.

Focus on Planning and Starting Small

Within the introduction of this post we talked about the snowflake and the seed. Both started small, and yet both had BIG ideas that took a little time to cultivate and grow. The same applies to real life. We must think big but focus on planning and starting small.

Focus on ONLY What Want

Those who think big are solution oriented thinkers who only focus on what they want to do, have, be and achieve. They don't care about the details at first, or on what cannot be done. Instead they focus on the big picture and on the possibilities of bringing an idea to fruition. Later however, they ask effective ꝏuestions that breaks down their idea into workable parts — making them practical in real-life scenarios.

Focus on Highest Value Activities

Big thinkers always attempt to maximize the use of their time. As a result they primarily focus on only the highest value activities that will help them to bring their BIG ideas into reality.

Focus on Your Abilities and Strengths

When conceptualizing BIG ideas, big thinkers take into account their personal strengths and abilities. They realize that by conceptualizing ideas that naturally support their strong attributes and talents, that they will be able to bring forth more motivation and dedication to bring their ideas to fruition.

Consistently Reframe Problems

Those who cultivate the habit of thinking big consistently reframe their problems by expanding possibilities and perspectives. In other words, they first see the problem for what it is, then they twist their perspective of the problem in a creative way to help them brainstorm better ideas and solutions.

Consistently Surround Self with Ambitious People

Finally, big thinkers associate with other big thinkers who are ambitious, motivated and inspire others to think BIGGER, act BIGGER and become BIGGER than they ever imagined was possible.

The Barriers to Thinking Big

Thinking big is not easy. It's something that we must learn to cultivate over time on a daily basis in everything we do. However, even when this habit of thinking big is deeply ingrained into our psyche, there will still be times when barriers will need to be overcome, obstacles will need to be surpassed, and old habits will need to be broken. It is during these times that we need to think big and do bigger things than ever before.

Here is a list of common barriers that prevent big picture thinking:

Limiting Habits

Thinking big is a habit that we naturally grow and develop over time. It is a habit that allows us to stretch our imaginations and expand our personal potential. This is all well and good, however, thinking big will never become a reality for any of us if we continue to indulge in the following limiting habits that ironically force us to think small:

• Procrastination holds you back and pulls you away from moving forward in your life.

• Short-term thinking denies you the ability to see solutions that lie a few steps ahead.

• Negative thinking prevents you seeing things that are possible to do now and in the future.

• Making excuses focuses you on what you don't want to do, be, have and achieve.

• Solving insignificant problems distracts you from what's most important and from the BIGGER picture.

• Over-analyzing things wastes time and energy on small matters that are of little significance.

• Seeking perfection forces you to dabble in things over and over again in an attempt to achieve the impossible.

These habits will constrict your ability to think big about your life and circumstances, because they force you to think small, to think about insignificant events and circumstances in unproductive ways, thus draining all your creative energies from the inside out.

Peer Judgment and Criticism

People judge what they don't understand or can't comprehend. Your BIG ideas and solutions can help change your life, can help change someone else's life, and as far as you are concerned, they can also help change the world. Not everyone will see things your way, and not everyone will believe what you see, however this shouldn't stop you from thinking big and bigger than ever before about your life conditions and circumstances.

People will always judge, criticize, condemn and complain. It's just a natural part of human nature. However, this is not a barrier to thinking big unless you make it so.

Common Fears

Our fears of change, success and failure can make thinking big very difficult to do. We worry about what lies in the future, we stress about not getting things right, and we concern ourselves with worst-case scenarios. These fears constrict us and coil us into a ball of small thoughts, decisions and actions — effectively warding off the habit of thinking big.

Life is about making mistakes, it's about taking chances, and it's about thinking big about your life and circumstances.

Year from now, when you are sitting on your rocking chair at 100 years of age — you sit there with a smile on your face, having no regrets. Yes life might not have gone exactly the way you imagined, but you smile because you thought big, took chances and enjoyed the journey. And that's what life is really all about, isn't it?

Having No Time or Incentives

When you are pressed for time you begin thinking small and only about things in the immediate future. Thinking big requires time, it requires dedicated attention and self-discipline that forces you to spread your horizons and open your mind to new possibilities and ideas. If you simply can't find the time to think big then you will always live small.

If you live life without any incentives, then there will simply be no motivation to stretch yourself emotionally or physically. Without motivation you will think small and neglect the BIGGER picture.

How thinking small influence your success

Good thoughts and actions can never produce bad results, bad thoughts and actions can never produce good results." James Allen

Thinking small to some individuals is a way of life, some people are so obsessed with it, sincerely it not their fault. The human brain is built to think small because our brain will always try to protect us from any danger why? Thinking big means steping out of your comfort zone.

In order to experience more in life, we have to enlarge our thinking. If thinking small thoughts produces small results, then the same principle applies to thinking big thoughts. What kind of thoughts fill your mind every day? If your mindset focuses on sickness, lack, barely getting by and mediocrity that is precisely what your life will produce.

I am not saying you can simply think your way of out a negative situation. Those larger thoughts must be put into action. I am saying that thinking positive thoughts produces hope, a confident expectation that will keep your dreams alive. When you expand your thinking, you expand your opportunities.

Countless numbers of individuals are unhappy with the life they are living, and yet nothing seems to change for them. One of the primary reasons they don't achieve their dreams is the failure to change their thinking, we are all design to think small but in order to achieve great result in life we have to change that. Successful people demonstrate the results of successful thinking.

Good thinking increases your potential. If your thinking shapes who you are, then it naturally follows that your thinking, big or small, determines your potential. Achieving that potential comes from making progress, which is often just one good idea away.

Jack Welch , former CEO of General Electric, once said, "The hero is the one with ideas". For many people, the greatest obstacle to their success tomorrow is their thinking today.

Establishing a new habit in any area of life requires diligence and discipline, and it definitely applies to successfully changing your thinking patterns. Albert Einstein once said, "The problems that we face today cannot be solved on the same level of thinking we were at when we created them."

Victor Hugo said, "An invasion of armies can be resisted, but not an invasion of ideas."

Unsuccessful people focus their thinking on survival, that small thinking. Successful people focus their thinking on progress. 95% of accomplishing anything is knowing what you want, and then paying the price to make it yours.

Thinking differently doesn't cost you anything, but it will require restraint when your thoughts begin sliding back into the old patterns. You can adjust your thoughts in the car, sitting on the couch, or even in the shower. Unfortunately, not thinking differently comes with a price. The creation of the automobile began with a thought. Men have walked on the moon because of greatly expanded thoughts. The cure for cancer and HIV/Aids will be discovered because someone will expand their thinking.

Stop small thinking and you will cease to limit what you can have, and what you can achieve. Open up and expand! There is an exciting future waiting for you! Start thinking big.

how thinking small compared you to the likes of grasshoppers,sloths etc

We subconsciously hold back because we're afraid of the disappointment and embarrassment of failing, even though we gave our all.

We may not notice that we're doing this, but chances are we do it more than we think. It's understandable, really. Nothing feels worse than trying our hardest and still seeing that it's not enough. Rejection hurts, and just like any cold shoulder or eye roll at a club, this can get us down. So instead of risking the pain, we decide we'd better hold back because then at least we'll avoid rejection. But this defense mechanism will ultimately do nothing more than hold us back from our greatest potential.

We spend too much time thinking about Plan B and Plan C, instead of focusing all of our energy on Plan A why? Because we think small like sloths.

Nothing is wrong with having a backup plan. The problems only arise when said backup plan is more thorough than our original plan. The energy we use to protect ourselves in this way can oftentimes prevent us from success that could have been ours. We need to give our ideas and creations all the love and attention that they need, and focus on an escape route if and when we need one, guess who thinks this way a grasshopper.

We think we've failed if we didn't meet the exact goal that we set out to accomplish — essentially, we overuse the word failure.

"I didn't get the job, so I failed." Sure, not meeting our original goals can feel a lot like failure, but to accept this discredits all of the work and growth we experienced in the process. While we didn't get the job, maybe we learned what some of our weaknesses are, and what our strengths in the application process were. Now we can use these to our advantage for the next opportunity — the one that's really meant for us. In general, we need to stop crippling ourselves with the word failure, that word is for the fools. We need to change our thinking and stop thinking like a grasshopper or slothes.

Grasshopper see the glamour of success in all fields, but forget about the hard work.

Everyone dreams about working at the top of their respective field, whether that be Vogue for fashionistas, the NFL for footballers, or Thought Catalog for writers, and so on and so forth. What our dreams always leave out, unfortunately, is the hard work. Despite the fact that we live in a hyper-connected world where editors, recruiters and scouts are just a tweet away, the reality of reaching our dreams is farther away than ever before. Our dreams can feel so close and tangible, but allowing ourselves to get lost in the magic of passion will ultimately get us nowhere unless we change our thinking.

A small thinker simply strive to be like other people, instead of being the best version of ourselves.

At the end of the day, we should never try to be someone else. Maybe we see a particular personality type doing well in the world — rude and first-world-complain-y people on social media, for example. But trying to succeed by mimicking them will never lead us to happiness. We'll only reach emotional, mental, and professional satisfaction by defining, building, and sharing ourselves. Let's remember it this way (regardless of how simple or dumb it may sound): Pepsi will never be the best Coke, and Coke will never be the best Pepsi — so all they can do is develop and change to be the best Coke and Pepsi that they can be.

How thinking big compared you to the likes of lion, wolf, eagles, tigers etc

So, to be succinct, think like a wolf and be true to your values and the capacity for weakness vanishes. Think like an ape and make excuses, seek justifications for your actions, and suffer the fate of being a deceiver. Be that ape and you are casting an imaginary vote for a world and society where deception is law: where virtue goes to hell for self-gain. If what you hold dear is material gain and power, then maybe deception is your game.

To quote philosophy writer, Mark Rowlands, in his book "The Philosopher and the Wolf", he states "The weakness we manufacture in ourselves consists, fundamentally, in a certain way of thinking about ourselves and the evil acts we commit. We whine our excuses; we snivel of our extenuating circumstances. We couldn't have done otherwise, we tell ourselves and anyone else who will listen. Perhaps this is true. But our weakness consists in thinking that this matters. A lion does not make excuses. A wolf does what it does – perhaps what it has to do – and accepts the consequences."

We, being the intelligent social creatures that we are, are capable of twisting stories and memories and lying to ourselves and each other. When we do something that may be evil (define evil I know), we twist the truth and comfort our actions with justifications. This is something wolves are incapable of doing. I am not saying to be exactly like a wolf, I am saying we need to stop lying to ourselves and each other. I am talking about the deeper lies, not surface lies like "I didn't cheat on you" or "I didn't eat that sandwich in the fridge." The lies that dig so deep that you are afraid to face them because they make you see the damage you have done or will do.

If I asked you for a favor, as a complete stranger, would you help me? Or would you ask for one good reason why you should help me?

See, reasons are for people who seek self-gain: What's in it for me? Right? It's all about labels and gains vs losses... everything is about numbers and reputation. It's about having more and not being more. It's about what you get and not what you give. If someone needs help... is that not reason enough? We always search for meaning in things and we look for reasons to do something. What is the meaning of my life? Why should I do this? What will I get out of it? Everything becomes a zero-sum game, a dirty competition, a bunch of debts and "I owe you's" to be paid. Don't wait for reasons to do things, if you care about it and it feels right, go do it. You are not a grasshopper so don't think like one. Life is meant to be lived, why search for happiness and meaning, when happiness is the way and meaning is irrelevant.

How the way you think (either big or small) determine how your life turns out

Thought power is the key to creating your reality. Everything you perceive in the physical world has its origin in the invisible, inner world of your thoughts and beliefs. To become the master of your destiny, you must learn to control the nature of your dominant, habitual thoughts. By doing so, you will be able to attract into your life that which you intend to have and experience as you come to know the Truth that your thoughts create your reality.

For Every Outside Effect There is an Inner Cause: Every effect you see in your outside or physical world has a specific cause which has its origin in your inner or mental world. This is the essence of thought power. Put another way, the conditions and circumstances of your life are as a result of your collective thoughts and beliefs. James Allen said it best when he said "circumstances do not make a man, they reveal him". Every aspect of your life, from the state of your finances to the state of your health and your relationships, is accurately revealing your thoughts and your beliefs.

It's an Inside Job: Most people have it back to front, believing that they feel or think a certain way because of their circumstances, not knowing the truth that it is their thought power that is creating those very circumstances, whether wanted or unwanted. By internalizing and applying this Truth, that your thoughts create your reality, you will grant yourself the power to create the changes you want to see manifest in your life. Reality creation is an inside job.

Your Thought Power is Limitless: There is a single, intelligent Consciousness that pervades the entire Universe, which is all powerful, all knowing, all creative and present everywhere at the same time - the Universal Mind. Your mind is part of this One Universal Mind and since your thoughts are a product of your mind, it follows that your thought power too is limitless. Once you truly understand that your mind is one with the Single Source of All Power and that this power is within you, you will have found the only true source of infinite power for which nothing is impossible and impossible is nothing. Know that thought power comes from within. Accessing the source of All Power starts by looking inwards.

Your Thoughts are Alive: The greatest mystics and teachers that have walked the Earth have told us that everything is energy. This has now been undeniably confirmed by modern science. Your thoughts too are energy. William Walker Atkinson told us that "where mind is static energy, thought is dynamic energy - two phases of the same thing" and Charles Haanel went on to say that "thought power is the vibratory force formed by converting static mind into dynamic mind". Your thoughts are alive. Each time you entertain a specific thought, you emit a very specific, corresponding frequency or energy vibration.

Not All Thoughts Are Created Equal: The attractive power of any particular thought is determined by how often you have that thought, how big or small it is and by the strength of the feelings or emotions associated with it. The more energy you give to a particular thought, the greater its power to attract its corresponding circumstance into your physical world through the Law of Attraction. Your one-off, passing thoughts do not have the same creative power as your habitual thoughts and beliefs. Remember, that it is of little use to entertain positive thoughts for just a short burst of time each day if you then proceed to think negative or think small for the rest of the day. A negative thought cancels the benefit of a positive thought and vice versa. Since your reality is the sum total of all your thoughts there are many factors influencing your life. This makes it difficult to directly join the dots between the cause (thought) and the effect (circumstance) but the causation is always there.

Use the Power of thinking to Change Your Life: It is your subconscious mind that is the storehouse of your deep-seated beliefs and programmes. To change your circumstances and attract to yourself that which you choose, you must learn to programme and re-programme your subconscious mind. The most effective and practical way to do so, is to learn the simple process of creative visualization. It is the technique underlying reality creation, making use of thinking power to consciously imagine, create and attract that which you choose. Your imagination is the engine of your thoughts. It converts your thinking power into mental images, which are in turn manifested in the physical realm.

Become Aware of Your Thoughts But Not Obsessed: It is important that you learn to be aware of your habitual thoughts and to appropriately adjust them so as to maintain an overall positive mental attitude. However, be careful not to become obsessed with every thought that enters your mind as this would be equally counter-productive, if not more so, than not being aware of them at all. Remember that to obsess over your negative, unwanted thoughts, is to give them power and as the saying goes, what you resist persists. So instead of resisting any of your negative thoughts, simply learn to effortlessly cancel them by replacing them as they arise.

Tame Your Dominant Thoughts and Your Random Thoughts Will Follow Suit: It is estimated that the average person has between 12,000 and 70,000 thoughts a day. This is evidence enough to suggest that your goal should not be to control every thought. It is your dominant thoughts and beliefs that you must learn to bring under your conscious control as they are what largely determine your mental attitude. As you do, you will find your random thoughts themselves becoming more positive and more deliberate.

"All that we are is the result of what we think. The mind is everything. What we think we become."

In a nutshell, your life is the perfect mirror of your thinking, beliefs and dominant mental attitude. Whether you realise it or not you are already creating your reality through your thinking power. Every effect you see in your outside world has its original cause within you - no exceptions. To gain access to the greatest creative power at your disposal, you must learn to control the nature of your thinking, do I think big or do I keep thinking small. Your thoughts create your reality - know, internalize and apply this Truth and you will see your life transform in miraculous ways

Can anyone deny that bloodless battles rage around us every day, often fought against familiar enemies that loom from the past? The cause of these everyday battle wounds vary: a bitter divorce, the loss of a loved one, financial problems, unemployment, health issues, and the list goes on and on. However, one thing is certain; these emotional casualties sustained on the battlefield of everyday life can be as devastating to your long-term well-being.

It's easy to become overwhelmed and crushed by a negative situation, and to give up before you give yourself a significant chance to rebound. It's at these times that you are at your most vulnerable; your emotional warning system is at red alert and you can easily enter the negative zone where it seems like the entire world is against you.

- My life isn't working. (Boom!)
- I'll never live my dream. (Bang!)
- I'll never find someone who will love me for who I am. (Incoming!)
- I don't have what it takes to handle this. (It was really an honor to serve alongside myself.)
- My life is one big mess. (We are sorry to inform you that your confidence is dead. There was nothing we could do.)

This constant bombardment of fearful negative thoughts and words explode with tremendous force in your subconscious cause you to see a reality that you believe to be true. The result: You have lost the battle. You have let your defenses down and your life has been taken over by your own rogue thoughts and words, and you are vulnerable to hopelessness.

I'm not passing judgment on anyone who allows dark moments to take control of their emotions (I've been there myself at times). Certainly there are valid reasons for bad feelings to occur during difficult times, and it takes an incredible amount of fortitude to give thanks for the good things when so much is lost. However, if you expect to prevail during tough times, you must understand that it is your current perception of the situation that either gives you hope or makes you want to give up to a lost cause. If you're always thinking about how badly life is treating you, if you are always telling stories about how you can't get a fair shake, you will always feel miserable.

Ever hear the old saying, "Misery loves company"? Being miserable doesn't exactly attract good things, does it? If you want to change your life for the better, start by consciously changing what you think and how you think.

How to change the way you think

In an ideal world, our thoughts, experiences and beliefs would remain in a continuous state of refinement and renewal. We would frequently be exposed to new and interesting people and situations, and we would constantly discover and enhance new aspects of our emotional and intellectual lives.

However, this is rarely how life progresses. For many of us, personal ruts and situational repetition are the norm. Our focus narrows to daily stressors and events outside of our control. Our careers slowly push ahead, our circle of friends holds steady or shrinks over the years, and we content ourselves with familiar forms of recreation, mental stimulation and social interaction.

Then, one day, we wake up feeling we need something ... different. Perhaps we tire of dwelling on old worries or lost opportunities. Maybe we get bored of doing the same thing day after day. Or possibly we just want to see the "old" world in an entirely new way.

Whatever the reason, it's not hard to change the way we think -- but it does take some effort. What are some ways you can change the way you think?

Some people believe that the best way to help yourself change the way you think is to tell yourself -- repeatedly -- to think a different way.

The idea isn't new. In fact, it's very, very old. Most religious practices involve the repetition of prayers, appeals or affirmations. Militaries across the world demand that recruits change the way they think, and use chants, cheers and oaths to help do so.

You may decide to choose a very specific mantra -- "Public speaking is fun!" -- or something a little more broad, such as "Live in the moment." As long as your mantra or affirmation isn't grounded in the status quo ("Nothing must change, nothing must change"), it may help you change the way you think.

But choosing a mantra isn't enough. It's important to take time each day to review and repeat the catchphrase, or you won't give its message time to sink in. Try to repeat it throughout the day whenever a situation presents itself that challenges you.

Next: Do differently, think differently.

Trying to change the way you think? Why not try changing the things you do? It's not easy to change your perspective on things, especially when you're doing the same old things over and over.

Even making little changes in your life can help. Pick up a new sport or activity that you've always wanted to try. Go to restaurants, parks and other gathering places that you don't normally frequent. Try out a new author or musician, see a movie screened by your local film society, attend a community potluck, volunteer at a nonprofit, or attend a religious service that is different from your own.

Are you something of a "control freak"? Farm out tasks to others and set aside your high expectations and instinct to take the project over and do it your way. If you're more of a passive person, make an effort (even if just for a day or a week) to take matters into your own hands and to be more assertive. Introverts, attempt to come out of your shells. Commit yourself to initiating and maintaining a five-minute conversation with a total stranger once a day.

By changing or breaking even small routines, your brain will be exposed to new stimuli and will create new neural pathways to accommodate changes.

You must know how you think in the first place in order to think differently,

We can't think differently if we don't pay attention to the way we currently think. It isn't hard to walk through life with unchallenged or outdated beliefs, preconceptions, wrong assumptions and a personal narrative that's badly in need of updating.

Many people are afraid of acknowledging and exploring their own thoughts and emotions, choosing instead to focus on life outside their own skin -- the needs of others, career goals that have been set, and the constant static of the Information Age. Focusing on self-awareness can help you reconnect with your true needs, desires and dreams. It can make you pay attention to how you treat people and how you feel about how you're treated by others.

It may seem almost indulgent to work toward becoming more self-aware, but if so, there's nothing wrong with splurging on yourself. Increased self-awareness can facilitate major life changes -- the processing of painful events from the past, and the acknowledgment of resentments and fears in order to overcome personal demons and addictions. Identifying your moods and emotions will make it possible to adjust them. You can't change the way you think until you understand what's causing you to think the way you do.

To bring new thoughts, ideas and perceptions into your life, get to know someone with a different perspective, occupation, background, culture or religion.

Why? Hanging out with like-minded people is a good way to hear constant reinforcement of your own thoughts and beliefs. This also makes it easy to fall into "groupthink" and makes it more difficult to see faults, shortcomings and falsehoods of our own.

That's not to say you need to get rid of old friends -- just spice up your life with some new ones. New friends and acquaintances increase the odds that you're introduced to new ways of thinking. You may be pleasantly surprised to have your worldview rocked a little bit by a simple conversation with somebody who views life much differently than you do. The great thing about widening your social circle is that new friends can help expand it even further by introducing you to people you might otherwise have little opportunity to meet.

You don't have to travel to exotic lands to meet new people who think differently than you do -- in fact, they're all around you. It may just be a matter of being willing to initiate conversations with people from whom you'd normally shy away.

Next: change the way you think by changing the places you think

Going about your life the same way day after day, doing the same activities you've always done, and planning the next weekend to mirror the last one is a good recipe for shrinking your awareness, joy and understanding of the world.

We have a natural (and often useful) tendency to stick with the familiar in life and avoid situations that make us uncomfortable. This is a good way to stay out of sticky situations, but it's also a good way to get in a rut and stay there. Pushing yourself to embrace new activities and experiences that force you to step outside your comfort zone is a good way to change the way you think.

Perhaps it's something physically intimidating, like skydiving or bungee jumping. Maybe getting outside your comfort zone means you seek out public spaces in which you're an ethnic, cultural or religious minority. Instead of vacationing in well-worn tourist traps, try a new destination that's off the beaten path.

Now that we've gotten you on the path to seeing things a whole new way, thinking a whole new way.

I hope that you make good use of everything you read in this book and start thinking big

Conclusion

It is reasonable to expect that big thinkers don't always realize their BIG Ideas. However, what they do realize is that life doesn't always get them what they want, but rather what they need — in the long-term — to help support the achievement of their BIGGEST goals and objectives. Likewise, they understand that thinking big is not something that just happens to us, nor is it an attitude about life. It is rather a state-of-mind that we must choose to cultivate on a daily basis that becomes our life's attitude over a lifetime.

Disclaimer

This book is not intended as a substitute for the medical advice of physicians. The reader should regularly consult a physician in matters relating to his/her health and particularly with respect to any symptoms that may require diagnosis or medical attention.

(selfhelp,success)

ABOUT THE AUTHOR

My name is MARY DAVENPORT, I am the founder and owner of THE ACT OF CREATIVITY (TAOC).

I am first and foremost a mother of 3, grandmother of 8. Have been freelancing for many years now , as a writer before I setup my own organization, i am also currently an hotel general manager and an avid reader..my favorite is kindle publishing though..lol I really love educating people on how to become successful in life, stay healthy and live the life of their dreams

Do not go yet; One last thing to do

If you enjoyed this book or found it useful I'd be very grateful if you'd post a short review on it. Your support really does make a difference and I read all the reviews personally so I can get your feedback and make this book even better.

Thanks again for your support!

www.ingramcontent.com/pod-product-compliance
Lightning Source LLC
Chambersburg PA
CBHW031501210526
45463CB00003B/1022